WRITERS

ON

WRITERS

Published in partnership with

WRITERS
RICHARD
COOKE
ON
ROBYN
DAVIDSON
WRITERS

Black Inc.

Published by Black Inc.
in association with the University of Melbourne and State Library Victoria.

Black Inc., an imprint of Schwartz Books Pty Ltd
Level 1, 221 Drummond Street, Carlton VIC 3053, Australia
enquiries@blackincbooks.com
www.blackincbooks.com

State Library Victoria
328 Swanston Street, Melbourne Victoria 3000 Australia
www.slv.vic.gov.au

The University of Melbourne
Parkville Victoria 3010 Australia
www.unimelb.edu.au

9781760642303 (hardback)
9781743821329 (ebook)

A catalogue record for this
book is available from the
National Library of Australia

Cover design by Peter Long and Akiko Chan
Photograph of Richard Cooke: Loulou
Photograph of Robyn Davidson: Kym Smith / Newspix
Text design by Peter Long
Typesetting by Akiko Chan

Printed in China by 1010 Printing.

To my grandfather

πρὶν δ᾽ ἂν τελευτήσῃ, ἐπισχεῖν, μηδὲ καλέειν κω
ὄλβιον ἀλλ᾽ εὐτυχέα

A few hundred years hence, in this same place, another traveller, as despairing as myself, will mourn the disappearance of what I might have seen, but failed to see.

Claude Lévi-Strauss, *Tristes Tropiques*

1

SETTING OUT

Maatsuyker Island, a sea-worn islet off the southernmost coast of Tasmania, is among the most remote places in Australia. It is inhospitable – permanent gales sometimes raise surrounding waves to a twenty-metre swell – but not un-inhabited. It has a lighthouse, still operated by volunteer lightkeepers who sign on for a season of isolation. They spend it maintaining the mechanism, flying kites and noting down rare clouds for the Bureau of Meteorology.

Esther Nunn was the lightkeeper on Maat-sukyer Island when she first encountered Robyn Davidson. A friend sent her *Tracks* (1980), which arrived via helicopter, and on its cover was a photo of the author, atop a camel, in front of Uluru. *I want to do that*, was the lightkeeper's first thought.

Esther Nunn spent her thirtieth birthday on the desert sand of the Gunbarrel Highway in the Northern Territory, naked and leading a file of camels. It was 2010, and she was 101 days into a tribute trek to mark the thirtieth anniversary of *Tracks'* publication. 'That book became my bible,' Nunn told me, and her copy – she still has the chopper-delivered original – is full of underlining and asterisks. As she made a version of Davidson's passage from Alice Springs to the Coral Coast in Western Australia, she compared the places described in the book to the places she was seeing, and tried to visualise how the country had changed. After 162 days, she reached the waters of Shark Bay.

She wanted to keep her camels, and so, in time, walked back across the desert to Alice Springs. This round trip took the best part of three years.

Calling a book or an author 'life-changing' doesn't say much: all literature is life-changing, if the increment of alteration is mundane enough. But the capacity to reach out to a far-flung ocean rock, population one, and turn that lone reader into a cameleer and desert pilgrim – what would you call that? Esther Nunn calls it life-defining, and her experience, while pronounced, is not unique.

Anna Krien's lifelong attachment to Robyn Davidson began the same way: with a photo. 'I remember being in a pizza shop when I was a kid, seven or eight maybe,' Krien told me, 'and the *National Geographic* with her on the cover was there, and I swiped it. She felt important. And my hunch was right. Her desire to just be alone when she went into the desert resonated with me.' Davidson has since become a 'moral compass' for Krien in her writing, though she thinks she 'lacks the same bravery'.

A similar image of Robyn Davidson was the accidental starting point of this essay. This time, the woman entranced was my wife, Loulou. We had travelled to Alice Springs because of Bruce Chatwin (a symmetry – Bruce Chatwin had travelled to Alice Springs because of Robyn Davidson), and there, in Red Kangaroo Books, we chanced on a collection of Rick Smolan's photography, *Inside Tracks*. Lou, who grew up in China, had never heard of Davidson or her work. She knew only that the figure on the cover, waist-deep in water and holding a camel against a backdrop of sea and sky, was the most beautiful woman she had ever seen. (This was also the description of Davidson that Smolan used in interviews.) So we bought it, and we bought *Tracks* as well.

I watched as the power of this book and its author, their energy and weight, worked an entrainment across cultures and generations. 'I have never, or haven't for a long, long time, felt that kind of connection with anyone, in any material, or in any medium,' Lou told me later. 'It's hard to explain, but I am drawn to that solitude, or freedom in disguise as solitude.' It was a variation of the same sensation Krien and Nunn experienced, where Robyn Davidson became an avatar for their sense of freedom.

'She managed what I couldn't, what most couldn't,' was how Lou summed it up. 'And you can't just assume it's some kind of recklessness. I don't think about her culture and mine when I read *Tracks*. It's just a human thing. It's even rawer than that.'

Other writers, no matter their calibre, held no immunity against this effect. Doris Lessing received countless fan letters, but when a young Robyn Davidson wrote to her in 1977, Lessing responded. First, the future Nobel Prize winner encouraged the writing of *Tracks*, then suggested Davidson move to the United Kingdom, and finally put her up in the basement flat of the Lessing home while the book was edited. Bruce Chatwin spent years trying to articulate a homespun theory of what he called 'human wanderlust', and had already compiled a busy manuscript titled 'The Nomadic Alternative', which his publisher had rejected. After he met Davidson, and they talked over their shared interest in nomadism, Chatwin travelled to Alice Springs and met three of Davidson's friends: Jenny Green, Toly Sawenko and Petronella Waifer. Under assumed identities, they became the central characters of Chatwin's refreshed book about nomadism, *The Songlines*.

In return, Chatwin introduced Davidson to Salman Rushdie, and the two had a volcanic relationship. In his 2012 memoir *Joseph Anton* (named for the pseudonym he assumed in hiding, post-fatwa), Rushdie describes how years earlier, on a plane home from Sydney, 'his emotions running high after his first few overwhelming days with Robyn', he took out a black notebook and began making notes for a novel about migration, the 'disjointednesses of here and there, then and now, reality and dreams'. The novel would become *The Satanic Verses*. Its character Alleluia Cone is based on Davidson – she is reimagined as a mountaineer – and is perhaps the sole person in the book who has genuine access to the transcendent:

Allie kept to herself the knowledge that she must placate the mountain or die, that in spite of the flat feet which made any serious mountaineering out of the question she was still infected by Everest, and that in her heart of hearts she kept hidden an impossible scheme, the fatal vision ... the solo ascent.

So who is the person at the epicentre of all this seismic activity? She is a feminist icon, one of our most consequential authors and a unique individual. But perhaps we should start with something she is not: Robyn Davidson does not like to call herself a writer, or at least not a Writer.

This was self-deprecation, I thought at first, but her hesitancy was so pronounced and recurrent when we spoke that it had to be something more. A writer is 'the thing that I mostly am', she would admit, while a 'real writer' is someone 'who knows that's what they want to do – they know that's where their talent lies, and their ability. And I don't seem to have that.' A writer was someone else, in other words. After forty years and five books – one of which has sold more than a million copies – Davidson is still not sure that writing is what she is good at, or what she wants to do.

2

REMEMBERING FREEDOM

Castlemaine, Victoria, is the place that brought Robyn Davidson back from decades of exile in Europe and India. She has renovated a property there. She sometimes thinks of the house, once a burned-out pub, as an old girl she helped back up onto her feet. I could feel, almost see, all the guilt and pleasure of not writing folded into the house and garden.

'Really, the project of the last six years has been this house. Making a safe place, I guess,' she said. 'And that's been tied up with trying to finish the memoir and everything else. And once the home is completed, then I can fuck off.'

Others have commented on her attractiveness her whole life; to her it has become almost an in-joke. Suitors persist, locally – tradies, retirees, divorcees. One knocked while I was there – he interrupted, nervous, on a spurious errand with a cover story that fooled no one, and when he left, the odour of Jean Paul Gaultier cologne stayed, loitering in the hallway.

She took me on a domestic tour – desert-coloured interiors, a garden on an ambitious scale, camping gear still to be unpacked from her car – and said her favourite place in the house was the reading room. 'What I'm really interested in,' she said, 'is consciousness.' She pronounced the word carefully, as though clearing away the tang of bong smoke it had accrued in the 1960s.

She carried no literary ambitions in childhood. She trained, in adolescence, as a concert pianist. She grew up in the country, on a cattle station in Queensland, where music lessons were a link to the lost world of 'accomplishments', the means by which middle-class women became cultivated. She enrolled in music school but dropped out, and went to live in a squat with an abandoned piano. After time at the tail end of the Sydney Push, the bohemian enclave of 'critical drinkers' that also produced Clive James, Germaine Greer and Robert Hughes, she headed inland, seeking a different kind of elsewhere. Years later, she found herself at the keyboard once more. She still plays – 'badly', she says.

Dread and avoidance are common impediments to writing, but Davidson's degree of affliction is legendary. A deadline turns her into a flight risk. She has moved countries to avoid finishing a manuscript, and she still likens the act of writing to stage fright, performing a recital for which she has no sheet music, on an instrument she has forgotten how to play.

I made a guess, later confirmed, that Alfred Cortot would be one of her favourite pianists. Cortot hated practising, a habit that contributed to his famous tendency to make mistakes. His compensation was a life lived to the full, which enriched his interpretations of the Romantic composers, especially Chopin, imbuing them with emotion. His playing, even when frayed, was poetic.

Davidson is frank, almost harsh, about her technical imprecisions as a writer, but her calculus is similar. Writing is only a means to express what is most important to her, which is a desire for freedom. As often – more often – this desire takes her away from writing altogether.

I was conscious, in questioning Davidson

about her life and work, of how furrowed my path was. I lagged decades of writers and pilgrims, interlopers and fans. Reading interviews to try to chicane through the questions already asked was pointless. They most often sought answers about the same thing – her first book, now published forty years ago.

'You must have heard the word "tracks" tens of thousands of times. Perhaps millions of times,' I tried.

'A gazillion,' she replied.

I tried to fight *Tracks*. I read the rest of Robyn's work, seeking digressions and unorthodox openings, trying to reframe things. In the end this felt only avoidant, or artificial. There was no fighting it. She had walked the desert with camels, and this had come to define her.

Her account of the journey 'hit something mythic', as she put it.

A book was not part of the initial plan, but the duration of the trek – nine months – meant she needed money, for camels and supplies. *National Geographic* gave it to her, on the condition that she write about her experience.

The resulting article was called 'Alone', though she had not been alone the whole mission. Apart from her camels, and her dog, Diggity, she was accompanied intermittently by *National Geographic* photographer Rick Smolan, and an Anangu elder named Mr Eddie, who guided her past sacred sites. But the figure of the lone, questing woman was irresistible. She was famous before the desert crossing was completed – newspaper reporters sought her out while she was still miles from the coast – and at her destination she found a media-constructed persona already waiting for her: the 'camel lady'.

This character, or caricature, has been unusually durable – younger generations that do not know Davidson's work still know of 'the camel lady' – and she recognised the paradox almost immediately: her act of freedom, and its transmission to the public, would forever enclose her in a kind of iron maiden.

'Had I been a man,' she writes in *Tracks*, 'I'd be lucky to get a mention in the *Wiluna Times*, let alone international press coverage. Neither could I imagine them coining the phrase "camel gentleman". "Camel lady" had that nice patronizing belittling ring to it. Labelling, pigeonholing – what a splendid trick it is.'

In the popular imagination, she became a heroine: the opposite of what she wanted to communicate in the book. 'The point was,' she says, 'that anyone could do what I did.' Despite the camel-lady moniker, that was the message received by generations of writers, readers and travellers, especially women.

My friend James Young, a former cameleer turned shoemaker now living in Alice Springs, read *Tracks* during his own 2000-kilometre camel journey around far western New South Wales. He had followed the old stock routes from Bathurst to Forbes, and this experience gave him additional respect for Davidson as a cameleer. 'Robyn played a big game,' he told me. 'It takes confidence. It takes a lot of confidence to handle big animals, otherwise the anxiety goes onto them.' The world of cameleering in the 1970s was still overwhelming male, and attracted paranoiacs. Kurt Posel, the

Austrian camel trainer who spent two years terrorising and trying to swindle Davidson, was not an outlier in this world.

Until recently, James said, Alice was full of young people learning to cameleer. They would come looking to reinvent themselves, and slip into a continuum of knowledge that originated with the Afghan traders in the 1930s and 1940s.

His camel trip was formative. 'You find your own ways of living in the world,' he said, 'that's the dynamic.' Out there, 'you could invent how you were'. What he remembered was how long it took to pack – four hours on a bad day, when weather or camels were uncooperative – and the sensation of a family, a mutually dependent group of humans and animals. When his trip was over, he felt this loss of intimacy as a near-bereavement.

Davidson said that a stranger once approached her with a story. An acquaintance had read *Tracks*, it had had its effect, and she went off to travel the world. 'She was visiting Machu Picchu, this woman, and she stepped back to take in the view, and she fell off a ledge and died. That's what she told me,' Davidson said.

The woman who related this story said, 'I thought you'd like to know.'

'Camel trips, as I suspected all along, and as I was about to have confirmed, do not begin or end: they merely change form.' These are the final lines of both *Tracks* and its fortieth-anniversary postscript. At first I thought the repetition too neat, almost glib, but it indicates something deeper. Davidson must revisit these trips unendingly. The transition from book to film, for example, took twenty-three years and a parade of unsuccessful screenplays, in which Julia Roberts was cast as the lead, or Davidson's moment of spiritual reckoning was represented by her naked body held aloft on a sea of Aboriginal hands. That kind of thing.

She is fine with the 2013 film, in which Mia Wasikowska plays Robyn and Adam Driver plays Rick. She says it is a rendering that, so long after the events it depicts, 'does not have much to do with me'. What the film lacks, I think, is the beauty of the book. The screen version is inert, languid, as if shot by an Instagrammer on a road trip, using a vintage filter. It is too tasteful. When an elderly Aboriginal woman is beaten in the pub where Davidson works, the violence happens off-screen. In the book, the ugly sexism and racism is immediate: Davidson is declared a 'rape case' by pub regulars, and, after repeated encounters with would-be intruders, flees her lodgings when she discovers a turd on her pillow. It is like a feminist retelling of *Wake in Fright*.

These provocations not only reinforce her motives in leaving white Alice Springs; they also inform the book's beauty. It has that quality Baudelaire called 'circumstantial beauty': as well as relaying the ineffable and eternal, it carries and captures the spirit of its time. 'Beauty' is not the first word that comes to mind recalling mid-1970s Australia, aesthetically defined as it was by Paul Hogan, toothy glam-rock bands, featurist architecture and hirsute sportsmen in tight clothing, but even these transmit a sense of freeing from stricture. Davidson has called the residue of 1960s radicalism a 'listlessness' – 'I reacted against that listlessness by deciding to do this journey,' she told an interviewer – and that listlessness has a bohemian beauty.

Tracks took more than one route to acclaim: it is an animal story, a feminist text, an adventure tale, a lively political tract. But its momentum came from combining a place, a time, an event and a person in a brush with the transcendent. The Push had petered out by the late 1970s, partly because the Whitlam government's more-liberal orientation made a stance of permanent protest redundant. Its energy did not dissipate entirely, though. Some Push ideas were subsumed into the Me Decade and the New Age movement; others were maintained in a suite of progressive politics, a shedding of colonial values and a determined sense of self-actualisation.

Davidson cautions against nostalgia, but her best work mines a related, less clichéd emotion. It is something closer to grieving, for the political expectations and liberatory prospects that were set loose in the 1960s and 1970s, the time when, she writes, 'the status quo of the developed world was under radical scrutiny by its youth'. She described this timespan, and her own experience of it, in that anniversary postscript:

> We reacted against the closing in of the post-war nuclear family, its concern with safety and security, in particular its assumption that women should remain inside the domestic realm. We wanted to understand the political forces that shaped society, the injustices that allowed us material wellbeing while vast swathes of the world starved, the imbalance of power and opportunity between classes, races, sexes. But perhaps most importantly, for someone like me, nothing was as important as freedom. The freedom to make up your own mind, to make yourself. And such

aspirations inevitably involved risk, unleash-
ing opportunities for learning, discovering
and becoming.

I am describing a cliché of course, and
the reality was far more variable and compli-
cated (we were also spoilt and selfish). But
no one can live too far outside the clichés of
their time. I arrived in Alice Springs carried
at least in part by the momentum of that era's
sense of promise, quest and justice.

Tracks could not have been written by a mid-
career writer. It has awareness without self-
consciousness, and a fresh, vernacular voice.
A more jaded mind would not have been as
conductive. The Central Australian landscape is
not easy to capture on the page, and Davidson's
intimacy with the country provided startling
descriptions: a first home's 'nestling correctness',

conflicting emotions that reverberate 'like drums in a canyon'.

Doris Lessing gave a cover quote for the first edition: 'A strong, salty fresh book by an original and individual young woman. This will rank among the best of the books of exploration and travel and, like them, is a record of self-discovery and self-proving.'

The second half of this quote is reproduced often. I am not convinced that *Tracks* is a record of self-discovery, though. Part of the irreducible sense of freedom at the heart of the book comes from privacy: Davidson divulges something intimate without ever saying what it is. She had attempted an 'adventure of the mind, or to use an old-fashioned word, the spirit', and that spirit was also the spirit of an age.

That sense of freedom is what draws me to Robyn Davidson – not only to her writing, but to her way of being. She is not an obvious heir to the throne of bohemia, but among the Push legatees, she has kept more fidelity to the idea of creation as a way of living *against* than most of her contemporaries.

'I think hard times are coming,' Ursula K. Le Guin said, accepting an award in 2014, not all that long before her death, 'when we will be wanting the voices of writers who can see alternatives to how we live now, and can see through our fear-stricken society and its obsessive technologies to other ways of being.' Most important, she said, were 'writers who can remember freedom', writers who knew the difference between production of a market commodity and the practice of an art.

'The name of our beautiful reward is not profit,' Le Guin concluded. 'Its name is freedom.'

3

TRAVEL WITHOUT TRESPASS

A lesser book than *Tracks*, by a lesser writer, would have lingered on the motive for the desert crossing it recounts. Instead, Davidson leaves the 'why' largely undisclosed, unknowable even to her. Its origin seems to flow directly from her subconscious: while participating in an acting workshop in the early 1970s, she was asked, 'What is the substance of the world in which you live?' and was surprised to hear herself answer, 'Desert, purity, fire, air, hot wind, space, sun, desert desert desert.' This mantra is indivisible from the impulse that compelled her trip; it was a decision 'which carried with it things that

I could not articulate at the time'. A version of this reasoning can also be found in Wilfred Thesiger's 1959 book *Arabian Sands*. Thesiger found that travelling through the Empty Quarter of Arabia had 'little importance. It would produce nothing except a rather inaccurate map which no one was ever likely to use. It was a personal experience, and the reward had been a drink of clean, nearly tasteless water. I was content with that.'

There was one aspect on which Davidson was clear: the continental walk was not therapy. Her cosmopolitan mother, lonely and isolated, had committed suicide when Davidson was eleven, and this biographical detail has furnished amateur psychoanalyses of her ever since. Before she had even departed Alice Springs, Davidson was contending with 'astounding projections' from others, among them a belief that the journey was a means 'to do penance for my mother's death'. Her only serious disagreement with John Curran, the director of the film version of *Tracks*, was over his decision to include this maternal trauma, which does not appear in the book. 'The problem for me there,' she told an interviewer in 2014, 'is that the hidden message then becomes that for a woman to do anything extraordinary, she has to be disturbed in some way. She has to have something to work out.'

Her misgivings were prescient. Curran's stubbornness meant that an Australian critic could group his film with *Wild* and *Eat, Pray, Love* in a loose thematic trilogy, 'a series of notable solo filmic voyages by women seeking self-discovery, all drawn from best-selling memoirs'. Cheryl Strayed in *Wild*, 'like Davidson', is 'healing herself after the death of her mother'. This is just the crude Freudian diorama the memoir sought to avoid. Davidson has an uneasy relationship with this school of confessional travel writing. Elizabeth Gilbert's *Eat, Pray, Love* may not have been directly inspired by *Tracks*, but it too turns on a spontaneous decision by a solo traveller seeking the sublime. This has since become perhaps the dominant mode of contemporary English-language travel writing, reducing an already troubled genre to platitudes of the soul.

By the early 2000s, this style of narrative had taken the sentiment at the heart of *Tracks* – an exploration of consciousness – and commodified it into a reductive exploration of Western womanhood. In her essay 'How Not to Be Elizabeth Gilbert', the critic Jessa Crispin lamented this peculiarly gendered division, where 'men go on adventures, women on journeys of self-discovery'. Crispin dissected Gilbert's work, suggesting that *Eat, Pray, Love* had 'more in common with memoir' than with traditional travel tales. *Eat, Pray, Love*, she says, inspired a genre of 'faux travel writing' where 'the focus of attention is the self, and the beautiful locale becomes the backdrop of the real action, which is interior psychodrama'.

Consider this selection of synopses from Amazon:

> After graduating from college, Jennifer isn't sure what she wants to do with her life. She is drawn to the Appalachian Trail ... With every step she takes, Jennifer transitions from an over-confident college graduate to a student of the trail ... (*Becoming Odyssa: Adventures on the Appalachian Trail*)

Ornithologist Caroline Van Hemert began to feel stifled in the isolated, sterile environment of the lab ... she was compelled to experience wildness again. (*The Sun Is a Compass: A 4000-Mile Journey into the Alaskan Wilds*)

After college and a brief, disastrous marriage, Neva Sullaway attempts to escape her anguish as well as the post-Vietnam confusion of her generation by sailing alone around the world. (*Chasing Dreamtime: A Sea-Going Hitchhiker's Journey Through Memory and Myth*)

Compelled by a force she can neither articulate nor resist, a woman throws caution to the wind. Her family and friends object. The titles themselves have the duration of a micro-journey: *The Good Girl's Guide to Getting Lost:*

A Memoir of Three Continents, Two Friends, and One Unexpected Adventure and *The Lost Girls: Three Friends. Four Continents. One Unconventional Detour Around the World*. Even Davidson's own title was colon-ised – the American edition of *Tracks*, published in 1995, tacked on *A Woman's Solo Trek Across 1700 Miles of Australian Outback*.

Not surprisingly, Davidson resists these associations. She has a visceral sense of the laden history of the genre, for so long 'the voice of the centre talking over the subaltern', as she puts it. Neither anthropology nor ethnography, it is instead 'a waffly sort of genre that allows a lot of ill-thought-out stuff to go in there'. Among the most ill-thought-out are these confected journeys of self-affirmation, a pick-and-mix from colonised cultures, where the philosophical insights are reverse-engineered from the book contract. She has fought a rear-guard action against the self-help genre's slow conquest of travel writing.

There are also generational distinctions between these works. 'The wild' has become a different place these past forty years. Davidson believes it would be 'kitsch' and 'impossible' to attempt *Tracks*-style travel now, because the possibilities of privacy and freedom she experienced have been breached by telecommunications technology. 'I think what happens,' she said in one of our discussions, 'is that Western travellers or Westerners have a kind of innocence.' They romanticise certain folk ways, and those 'exquisite, beautiful houses and huts', without thinking that some locals might prefer a McMansion. Longings and nostalgia are projected onto other cultures. 'It becomes a very dodgy genre, and it's becoming more so.'

Tracks is distinguished, too, by its political sensibility. While some of its aspirations might now seem naive or patronising, most are still ahead of their time. Davidson had a desire for direct contact with Indigenous culture through country, and for part of the trail was guided by Mr Eddie, an elder from the Western Desert community of Wingellina (his daughter, the artist Jean Burke, later painted Robyn as the camel lady). Australia's treatment of its Indigenous citizens enraged Davidson, and media interest in her story offered a platform for polemic. In *Tracks*, she compares the situation to apartheid South Africa. In an interview with *The Australian Women's Weekly* in 1980, she refers to 'cultural genocide' committed against the Indigenous population. She says she sometimes feels the prospects for Indigenous peoples are worse now than they were then.

Aboriginal land rights were part of a lasting, if limited, legacy of postwar radicalism. 'After the sixties were over, there was this change of mood among our lot,' Davidson says. 'We had this notion that things could be changed, or that somehow the world would be a better place. Then it became obvious that the energy went out of that … That was when a lot of people went up to Alice Springs. Because they could be involved in that [land rights]. That was a real thing.' It was, she wrote in *Tracks*, a period when 'nothing was as important as freedom', but the freedom did not entail trespass. It was freedom grounded in an understanding of history and culpability, part of an incipient tradition in postcolonial literature that has been called 'anti-conquest'.

This awareness meant Davidson's 'vision' lent itself to interpretation through a critical lens. The scenery in *Tracks* is not a mere back-drop. Davidson's 'embryonic beginnings of that rapport' with unmistakably Australian country marked a turning point in Australian writing: a sincere engagement with and recognition of the zone for so long experienced as the country's 'dead heart'.

4

THE DEAD HEART

B y venturing into the desert, Robyn
Davidson was also entering a literary
landscape. It was a place imagined and
projected onto by the writers of settler Australia,
a site of anxiety seen as inimical to life. Art, literature and politics registered it most often as
a metaphysical absence: the concepts of *terra
incognita* and *terra nullius*, the unknown and
the unoccupied, were combined into a dreadful
blank.

The phrase 'the dead heart' is a distinctive
local colloquialism for 'the remote inland area
of Australia', according to the *Oxford English
Dictionary,* and its etymological origin is

another camel trek. When geology professor J.W. Gregory crossed what was then called Lake Eyre in South Australia in the first years of the twentieth century, he titled his account *The Dead Heart of Australia*. The metonymy stuck, and almost as soon as it was coined, this ominous description was being qualified. 'The term "dead heart of Australia" is naturally meant to refer to Australia only in a geographical sense,' London magazine *The Sphere* reported, reviewing Gregory's book in 1906, the year of its publication. 'With regard to the white race now inhabiting the continent, there is no dead heart of Australia.'

Gregory 'dwells on the generosity, honesty and intelligence' of the Aboriginal workers he met on a mission, the reviewer wrote, 'but regrets the probable extinction of the race'. Meanwhile, white labourers flourished 'without special clothing or precautions', becoming tanned. It was 'a sight which suggested that a "white Australia" is no idle dream, at any rate for the dry regions of the centre and the west'.

This 'sense of space', Davidson writes in *Tracks*, was 'frightening' and worked 'deep in the Australian collective consciousness'. The threat was quarantined by dividing centre from periphery. The distinction became imposing, lodging the bush as the default landscape of the Australian creative consciousness. Forests, while acting as a proving ground for the figure of the settler (and his family), also formed a protective barrier between the interior dead zone and the enlivened colonies of the coast. These were green enough to pretend at England, and so could form a threshold of civilisation. Even those who had travelled across the centre thought this way: Frank Clune, in his 1942 biography of Donald George McKay, *Last of the Australian Explorers*, could call one of the chapters 'Probing the Blank Space'.

Probes, when they happened, were alternately ironic, sentimental and bleak. In her 1937 book *The Great Australian Loneliness*, the journalist Ernestine Hill describes her own camel journey through the Arrernte lands near Lake Eyre. This sojourn into what she calls 'wild n____r country' nevertheless contains a hypocritical lament for the region's indigenous peoples, who by then had been forced onto Christian missions. She relates an incident when her travelling party is excited by the sounds of people on a rocky outcrop. Perhaps a tribe remains? Their tracker is 'vastly amused at our innocence. "No more!" he contradicted, with the flash of a grin. "Bowerbird makim yaki all-same blackfella."'

'To me it was a poignant little incident, ineffably sad,' Hill records. 'The birds of the country remember when its people are gone.'

Hill experienced the landscape as overwhelmingly hostile. To her eye the plains have a 'bleak awfulness', beyond which the 'sandhills menaced away'. Her descriptions draw from the imagery of Gothic horror, with travellers 'winding through a Hall of Mirrors, amid shadowy shapes and witch-crafts that belong to the brush of a Goya or the pen of an Edgar Allan Poe'. Sanity is preserved by blocking this out. One white man rips open mail with 'obvious English postage stamps' and

> without a word to us, he dived in, page after page, in rapt silence, while the mailman unpacked some papers and a package of patent medicine. Once he threw back his head

and laughed heartily. The Great Australian Loneliness sobered him up for a moment, but he answered us absently. His heart was in England.

Other hearts would sustain this pretence for decades. In *A Town Like Alice*, published in 1950, a character newly arrived in Alice Springs acclimatises by pretending she is somewhere else: 'In spite of its tropical surroundings and the bungalow nature of its houses there was a faint suggestion of an English suburb in Alice Springs which made her feel at home.' Nevil Shute describes hedged gardens framing 'English streets'. The Australianness of the natural land-scape must be blocked out to preserve this fiction of belonging: 'Shutting her eyes to the MacDonnell Ranges, she could almost imagine she was back in Bassett as a child. She could now see well what everybody meant by saying Alice was a bonza place.' Such was the colonial re-imagining of Central Australia in the 1950s: to 'see well', you had to shut your eyes.

Compare this to the opening paragraph of *Tracks*. It is a similar scene: Robyn Davidson, just disembarked from the train at Alice Springs, turns against the wind to look at the same Mac-Donnell Ranges. This 'line of mountains at the edge of town' gives rise to a reckoning: 'There are some moments in life that are like pivots around which your existence turns, small intuitive flashes, when you know you have done something correct for a change, when you think you are on the right track.' The ranges orientate her, not only physically but also spiritually.

Davidson soon discovers this act of seeing makes her an outlier. In the eyes of other towns-folk, the ranges are a 'prehistoric monster' that has 'a profound psychological effect on the folk below. It sends them troppo. It reminds them of incomprehensible dimensions of time which they almost successfully block out with brick veneer houses and wilted English-style gardens.' Davidson does not comprehend this incomprehensible dimension, but she does acknowledge it, and so begins a process of re-engagement with the 'dead heart'. This turning represents a restitution for Australian literature as well.

There had been earlier literary challenges to the conception of the interior as a 'dead heart'. Patrick White's 1957 novel *Voss* captures the Australian dread of the desert, but repositions it as a kind of holy awe:

'Everyone is still afraid, or most of us, of this country, and will not say it. We are not yet possessed of understanding.'

The Lieutenant snorted, to whom there was nothing to understand.

'I would not like to ride very far into it,' admitted Belle, 'and meet a lot of blacks, and deserts, and rocks, and skeletons, they say, of men that have died.'

This austere, parsimonious landscape stands as a rebuke to the 'Palladian facade' of coastal Australian hypocrisy. Johann Ulrich Voss's expedition becomes an act of truth.

Davidson, too, goes to the desert in search of spiritual refuge; her crossing is a flight from white society's philistinism, especially its sexism. She uses the phrase 'the dead heart' only once in the book, early and half-ironically, and this epithet is applied to the town, not the surrounding desert. Her first impression of Alice Springs is of 'the architectural ugliness of the place, a discomforting contrast to the magnificence of the country which surrounded it'. The sprawling suburbia is 'stopped short by the great perpendicular red face of the Mac-Donnell Ranges'. Unlike Shute's envisioning of the town, the mountains are an antidote to the 'soulless, rootless … Ku Klux Klan country'.

The desert poses less danger than the townsfolk. Davidson finds herself in a community 'where men are men and women are an afterthought', a masculine outpost addled with social tensions. Despite what local racists impress upon her, it is the white population who are threatening. They leer at her chest, and their late-night prowls to her room cease only when met with the barrel of an (unloaded) rifle. It was here on the frontier that 'the stereotyped image of the Aussie male is still so sentimentally clung to. The modern-day manifestation is almost totally devoid of charm. He is biased, bigoted, boring and, above all, brutal. His enjoyments in life are limited to fighting, shooting and drinking.' No wonder the 'mythological crucible' of the outback and its culture represents freedom.

During her trek, Davidson confronts the dread this landscape evokes in white Australia and finds new possibilities beyond. 'The openness and emptiness which had at first threatened me were now a comfort which allowed my sense of freedom and joyful aimlessness to grow,' she writes.

Most of the people huddle around the eastern seaboard where life is easy and space a graspable concept, but it produces a sense of potential and possibility nevertheless that may not exist now in any European country.

It will not be long, however, before the land is conquered, fenced up and beaten into submission. But here, here it was free, unspoilt and seemingly indestructible.

Travelling with Mr Eddie changes her perspective. 'He made me notice things I had not noticed before,' she writes.

Noises, tracks. And I began to see how it all fitted together. The land was not wild but tame, bountiful, benign, giving, as long as you knew how to see it, how to be part of it. This recognition of the importance and meaning of Aboriginal land strikes many whites who work in that country.

When she starts to hit grazing land near the west coast, she is appalled by its condition. It is 'civilised' Australia that is dead, she realises. The continent's heart is living, while the periphery has been degraded beyond recognition:

I arrived at Carnegie to find it abandoned and more desolate and depressing than I can describe. Suddenly, dramatically, as soon as I hit the boundary fence, the country was broken. Eaten out by cattle. Destroyed. I had been so in tune with the marvellous un- touched country I had been through that I felt this change like a slap. How could they do this? How could they overstock their country and, with the great Australian get- rich-quick drive, lay it bare. There was nothing, not a thing, for my camels to eat. I thought I had come through the worst part, only to find the true desert, man's desert, beginning.

Two young men help her and provide food, and she rages at them about the state of the land. The difference between the country on either side of the fence is 'like chalk and cheese', and she becomes flustered when they have no idea what she is talking about.

'Couldn't they see?' she laments, before realising that 'one needs to have one's eyes peeled, and one needs to feel part of the earth before it is possible to notice the difference'. Six months before, 'I probably would not have been able to see it either.'

5

RUBY DEVISON

'No man can live this life and emerge unchanged,' Wilfred Thesiger concludes in *Arabian Sands*. 'He will carry, however faint, the imprint of the desert, the brand which marks the nomad.' For Davidson, this imprint deepened into a theory of neo-nomadism. It found fullest expression in her extended essay *No Fixed Address: Nomads and the Fate of the Planet* (2006), though she had written about these ideas intermittently before then. Her thesis compares modern extractive culture with older, peripatetic forms of living, and asks which has done 'less damage to ourselves, the environment and our animal kin'.

No Fixed Address begins at her home in the Indian Himalayas, which also represents a bulwark against travel and movement. 'I love this place and would like to be buried here,' she writes. 'When I say "this place", of course I don't just mean the house and its setting. I mean the people who live around me.' By then her fascination had been pursued to a point of exasperation and defeat in the country that she made her home, on and off, for more than twenty years: India.

Davidson's relationship to India was indistinguishable from a personal relationship with the Rajasthani nobleman and politician Narendra Singh Bhati. They spent twenty years together, and the country and the man flowed into one another. 'In a way he was India to me,' Davidson said. Through understanding Narendra, she could better grasp his nation and culture, and he shared his intimate familiarity with the Indian psyche – his work meant he oversaw a small empire, part-feudal, part-modern.

Ten years were spent living together, much of it in a hill house in the Himalayas. Ten years were spent apart, the couple divided between India and London, talking on the telephone.

Narendra also did something no one else could: persuade Davidson to undertake another journey and write about it. For a decade after the publication of *Tracks*, publishers had angled for a follow-up, and she had refused them all. 'I resisted and resisted and resisted,' she said, until Narendra encountered her at a London dinner party and told her she looked worn out. She could come to India, he said, where she would be looked after, and could 'write that book about the nomads'. The book would become *Desert Places*, published in 1996, but the seed had been planted back in 1978, after a chance meeting with Rabari tribespeople at the town of Pushkar, on the edge of the Thar Desert.

The Rabari, who sometimes call themselves ghosts, are camel-herders by tradition. In their origin myth, they were fashioned from dust by Parvati, Shiva's wife, to tend to his dromedary herds. This confluence of camels and nomads is Davidsonian, and *Desert Places* could have been a ready sequel to *Tracks*, with the same contours applied to the subcontinent. Instead, it is an anti-travel narrative, a chronicle of qualified failure. It is a project about the impossibility of anyone, let alone Robyn Davidson, writing a story like *Tracks* again. 'The writing of the book for me was about coming to terms with the fact … that a particular kind of travel book simply cannot be written anymore,' she told an interviewer in 2004.

Davidson planned to accompany a band of Rabari on their annual migration, to make contact with a waning and imperilled way of life. Both *National Geographic* and a photographer would be in tow. The mission was continually interrupted or delayed. The Rabari were ambivalent, and on the road the enterprise became a punishment detail. Reviews of *Desert Places* tend to emphasise the author's privations: villagers pelted her with stones; she was stared at and followed. An uncharacteristic ineptitude with the language left her marooned in the throng. She almost caught tuberculosis and brucellosis, contracted a tapeworm, and her dog died (again).

Worst of all, these sufferings seemed to yield little understanding, instead adding another layer to the thickening confusion and loneliness. Davidson questioned her motives, and so did the Rabari. 'You have lakhs and lakhs of rupees and you have a jeep. Why do you want to live with poor people? Why do you want to walk?' they would ask.

'I never found a suitable reply to this,' Davidson wrote, 'but it did indicate how far from enviable they saw their own lives and how incomprehensible they found mine.' This 'nightmare of mutual awkwardness', the 'little moat between us, widening each day', compounded feelings of isolation and rootlessness that were present before the mission. In London, 'somewhere in the midst of that tremendous restlessness I had lost the sense of a gravitational centre, a place with which to compare elsewhere', and linguistic solitude splintered it further.

Davidson could have dressed up the unpleasantness as asceticism, bumps on the road to an ersatz enlightenment, as Elizabeth Gilbert does in *Eat, Pray, Love* with the dive-bombing mosquitoes that afflict her meditation sessions in an Indian ashram. Instead, Davidson's dire straits destabilise the whole narrative, which yaws under the strain. 'Memory is a capricious thing' is the first line in the book, and the narrator becomes not only unreliable in the traditional way, as a flawed conduit for factual experience, but an unreliable proxy for the reader as well. She refuses to pretend. 'The many fault lines appearing in [her] character' leave Davidson in a rage too strong to quell. 'The words "I hate India" did not fit with the person I thought I was,' she writes. 'Everything enraged me, but what enraged me most was the sense of hopelessness … a weight measured not just by mass but by time.'

This exasperation underscores the most problematic elements of the trip. Her presence in the badlands begins to seem ill-advised, an affectation, Marie Antoinette assuming the costume of a shepherdess. Davidson was by then the *memsahib* of a noble house, and when the despair becomes unbearable, her partner's servants could spirit her away by jeep to showers and linens.

One of these men, her appointed guide, is a constant irritant, but the same implacable, Indian way of doing things means he can't or won't be substituted. They are linked, like 'two one-eyed men', according to a local expression. The unseemly business of magazine contracts and photography briefs, usually soft-pedalled in such accounts, becomes paramount, a Beckettian motivation that functions when all others fail.

After months on two or three hours of sleep a night, Davidson cracks. She revolts physically and mentally, pulling herself and her project apart. Her discomfort turns feverish, and she develops a full-blown case of misanthropy. She howls at humanity, exhausted. 'If India was terrible, so was where I came from. Worse, because it was so spoilt, so comfortable, so oblivious, and that comfort purchased at the expense of countries like this one.' Countries leech on one another, a monstrous 'fucked' pyramid with the 'little toy Rabari men' at the very base. 'Everything I had done here was fraudulent and absurd. I knew nothing about the Rabaris and, even if I did, it would mean nothing to them.' She is perpetuating a sham for the 'doctors' waiting-rooms' where the copies of *National Geographic* will end up. By the end, she loathes her 'initial romanticism more than my present incapacity to deal with reality'. Her camels are sacrificed to this, killed by lantana poisoning.

The result is a counter-epiphany, an experience that can be fought only to a draw. 'For a long time I could not see how to write about my experiences,' she concludes. 'They were nothing but a series of disconnected events, without shape, without meaning. I had passed through India as a knife does through ice and it had closed behind me at every step. How does one write about failure?' The answer is to break open the flawed genre of travel writing and show its failings.

When *Desert Places* was published, a young Pankaj Mishra reviewed it for the Indian magazine *Outlook*. He was impressed enough to excerpt it years later in his anthology of foreigners writing on India, *India in Mind*. Davidson, he thought, had found a way out of a dead end. Western accounts of the Indian subcontinent had changed since the mid-twentieth century, but improved little. 'The blunt xeno-phobia and facile contempt of Paul Theroux has been shunted into obsolescence,' Mishra wrote, only to be replaced by 'the imperatives of polit-ical correctness [that] don't permit anything beyond the amusement-tinged condescension which is these writers' primary narratorial stance'. Davidson's contact with India, defined by friction, was different:

> [*Desert Places*] enacts the painful contradic-tions in the situation of the estranged for-eigner who, while seeking virtue in a pre-modern culture, is so severely under-mined by the actual physical and psycholog-ical process of entering that culture that she lapses into the worst aspects of her disowned cultural self – that is, she becomes a *memsa-hib*. The shame, guilt and self-reproach that

accompany these bizarre personality trans-formations occupy a large space in the book, and contribute to its rigorous honesty, its unflinching candour.

Davidson said something similar to me: 'We can't be innocent about that anymore, in the way we talk about other cultures.' *Desert Places* was for her 'the end of the possibility of a kind of approach to travel writing'. The book's coda restores a modicum of balance, after her frus-trations exhaust themselves into acceptance, if not peace. 'If the beauty I saw that evening on the rim of the talab – the blue Aravalli moun-tains, moonlight on water, the silhouette bicycles, the fires of the toy Rabari men – could be broken down into ugly elements, then the reverse was also true.' Her feelings for Narendra tie her to India, but she knows her compulsion to return will remain even after he dies.

Unfortunately, she was proven right. Narendra died in 2011, and Davidson keeps returning. The India that defeated her in *Desert Places* became something else. There was even an alter ego thrust on her: Indians sometimes struggled to pronounce her name, and took to calling her 'Ruby Devison'. 'I saw Ruby Devison would be a very good pen-name, a false name to write,' she says. 'Then I could write *The King and I*, in true Mills & Boon fashion. But that's not what's interesting. That's the surface thing that has nothing to do with what actually goes on.'

What is it like, Robyn Davidson's India? 'I probably haven't processed it yet really,' she says. 'I lived there for thirty years on and off, and I still don't understand it.' It has changed the way she looks at home. 'What strange experiences do is give different slant on your own place. It also just felt too big to me, and my life with Narendra was so extraordinary. So utterly without precedent.'

The Himalayas were their home, but 'because it was so separated, so discrete, it was like a sort of bubble where we could go together and have a life but it wasn't real'. It was 'sort of slightly illusory, like a game'.

She thinks about that house in the mountains. It was a kind of paradise. Lonely, remote, but paradise nonetheless. She planted a garden there, her first.

The journey to the house began by overnight train, then an hour-and-a-half drive up the mountainside to the village, then, after loading supplies onto ponies, another hour-and-a-half walk up to the house. Initially there was no phone, nor much electricity. It became more restful with a stone extension, and phone lines, and a huge diesel generator.

She remembers the great calm of being around Narendra. When he was there, everything was taken care of and everyone looked after. He had a competence so immense he was regal, and when you were in his orbit you were completely safe. More: understood. She remembers this former life with sadness, and with fondness – deep, deep fondness – for the people who worked for them. She sees the servants when she returns. It is a very odd relationship: intimate, but involving a chasm of separation.

In the morning they would wake her with hot tea, and afterwards she would walk in the mountains with her dog. Have breakfast. Write a bit. Draw a bit. She read all of Shakespeare's plays up there, and would wander around the jungles, talking to herself in iambic pentameter. A full day of being immersed in reading, in a way that feels almost impossible now that such uninterrupted time is hard to come by.

The servants did not understand the concept of a garden, the purpose of planting and growing something unproductive. They hated tending to plants they couldn't eat. She would work on the garden, then visit London for three months and return to find it 'all dead or washed away. Or frozen, or dug up by monkeys.' A crude, simian symbol for the impossibility of putting down roots. One of forty or more places she has lived, but one of the few the nomad could call a home, a real home.

Murray Bail told her that her memoir could be structured around these places, one section for each. Periods of life defined by houses. The Queensland homestead in Stanley Park, where she was raised. The Sydney squat with the piano. A stone cottage on a camel farm in Alice Springs. Nine months of desert sand and night sky. Doris Lessing's basement apartment. An East London flat, shared with the actor Julie Christie. A house on a hill in India. And now her home in Castlemaine, Victoria. They are the grammar of her life.

Her memoir is not structured this way.

6

UNFINISHING

Writers often treat their works in progress with superstition. Some of the methods develop into near-occult practices, with incantatory logic and vows of silence, as though speaking words instead of writing them will squander a manuscript to the wind. They approach one another's unfinished manuscripts with caution, and improvised etiquette. Professional courtesies. Diplomacy. Don't ask, don't tell.

It is impossible to engage critically with an unseen work, and in another essay it would not be necessary to record those traces that we can see. But the dark matter of Robyn Davidson's memoir is too massive to ignore. It has quantum properties, existing and not existing at the same time. It has an ISBN, for example: 0330480812. Differing publication dates litter the internet: 12 April 2002. 1 September 2006. 9 September 2003. One site lists 'first known date: 2000'. Some retailers offer it for sale, though it is never in stock. Piracy sites invite an impossible download. It has trouble getting its story straight.

You can almost hear the sound of scratching out between its varying titles: 'Self-Portrait of an Imaginary Mother'. 'Self-Portrait with Imaginary Mother'. 'Self-Portrait with Imaginary Mother – A Reluctant Memoir'. Together they make an ostinato.

Twenty years ago, Davidson published a piece about how impossible the book was proving to write (this may become its first chapter).

In 2006, she told *Sydney Morning Herald* journalist Jane Sullivan that she had wrestled with the memoir for six years, and found herself pinned. 'It kind of broke the bank ... I was struggling with the damn thing and commuting all over the world and not earning. I'd like to go back to it, I can see how to do it now. It was never an emotional difficulty, it was purely a technical problem.' She abandoned it, and the literary agent David Godwin flew to India to persuade her to take it up again. That was in 2012.

In 2014, *The Guardian* asked after its progress – how many years had it been delayed? – and Robyn let the bidding begin: 'Fifteen – let's say 10, that sounds more respectable.'

The earliest reference to 'Self-Portrait' I can find is an article in *The Age*, where Robyn tells an interviewer she has never felt so 'bereft' of a way to begin a book. 'I don't know whether that's because I'm very scared of the material or whether I'm aware that the memoir form is so difficult. I really want to get this right.' That was in 1996. The project has been a presence in her life for twenty-five years.

Late-career counterweights, unfinished or unfinishable masterpieces: literary history holds few of these as comforting precedents. There is Truman Capote's *Answered Prayers*, the novel he embarked on after *In Cold Blood* – commissioned in 1966; missed its revised and re-revised deadlines in 1968, 1973, 1974, 1977 and 1981; its early excerpts proved social suicide, its latter chapters were burned or never existed. Ralph Ellison's *Juneteenth*, his second novel after *The Invisible Man* – forty years of work, more than 2000 pages, 368 of which were published posthumously. Ellison claimed an irreplaceable manuscript was destroyed in a house fire; biographers have their doubts.

These kinds of books (and non-books) become made only of telephone calls and pleading letters, or get gigantism and live as desk-bound secrets. Robyn Davidson's memoir is real. In 2018, she published its beginnings in the literary journal *Brick*. The opening passage describes a childhood argument over gold sandals, and then:

> When I came home that afternoon, my mother was dead. This could be the beginning of a memoir – a curtain drawn aside to reveal the whole landscape of life as it exists inside my mind and no one else's. But although I know the gold sandals were real, that I wore them on a particular day and this led to an altercation with my mother on the

stairs, these facts exist as no more than an instant of sense perceptions filed in memory and encased as a kind of seed. The other details in the picture – the skirt, portfolio, lunchbox; the duration in which the scene unfolds; the walk through the kitchen; the inference that I understood, at the time, the import of my actions – these have been furnished by imagination. If I continued with the story, it would unfurl out of that seed, that moment, and its relationship to what-really-happened would become increasingly obscure.

She writes about the innocence of her narratorial presence in *Tracks*, the naivety and assuredness with which she could recount experiences, and the loss of that innocence, replaced by 'a policing self-consciousness'. Her attempt is something paradoxical, almost self-defeating: a memoir against ego.

'You must always be mindful that the ego lies and it's very hard to write against that, to be constantly examining your own ego and your own motives,' she told me. 'I am too self-conscious. Or too conscious, maybe.' Her early work was written with such confidence – 'too stupid not to be confident. I just wrote it. And of course, as you read more and think more and grow more and understand more, it becomes harder to speak.'

The memoir form is boring her. It has her chained to the first person, rattling the bars. 'Originally it was a kind of quest for my mother,' she said. Her mother's death – the point 'she's not there' in the narrative – compels Davidson to write about herself. It becomes a 'more regular sort of memoir, because if she's anywhere, she's in me. And then I end up talking about my life.' This, she believed, requires an 'ability larger than mine'.

After I asked after the memoir – I approached it with more delicacy than she did – Robyn became briefly unresponsive to my emails. *On the lam again*, I thought. The reality was chastening. She had fallen in the garden – caught her foot in a snare of loose wire and hit her head – and she emailed a self-portrait with her forehead bandaged, holding up a thin sheet of paper. Diagnosis: concussion.

I felt a pang of concern, and as it abated, I realised I had been approaching Davidson in the wrong way. I had, subconsciously, started to police her, siding with the publishers, studying time and motion, graphing the career, keeping mental accounts, sketching equations of published words per year. I had, as a reader, been wanting more – more writing, more books. But a Robyn Davidson who wrote more books under less duress, who inhibited the sense of freedom that has preserved her, would no longer be Robyn Davidson. The sanctity of what happened to her in the desert was real, and it marked her. Her novel *Ancestors* (1989), and many of her shorter pieces over the last quarter of a century, were all rehearsals for this. The private responsibilities it entailed – the solo ascent – were her business.

In her *Brick* piece: 'My mother always overestimated my talents. The job she has given me is beyond them. I fail her as consistently as Hamlet fails his ghost.'

When Esther Nunn told Robyn Davidson she would follow her in tribute, Davidson wished her well, but did not insert herself into the project. Instead, there was a distance, which Nunn felt she understood. 'I got the sense she had done so many interesting things since – she had had such an interesting life for those thirty years! – that *Tracks* felt like a long time ago, belonging to another person. It is separate and complete in its own sense. It doesn't need to go any further.'

It would have been so easy for Davidson to follow others' inducements, to write seven versions of the same thing. Instead she saw through to the confounding truth behind these entreaties: they were requests to have a unique experience twice.

'Originality is not an ingredient of poetry, it is poetry,' another Push member, Clive James, said once, and the same is true here.

When we next spoke over the phone, postconcussion, we picked up the thread of the memoir again.

'I don't want to just push up books,' she said. She was wary of adding to the pile of what she calls 'print noise'. 'I don't want to just write books for the sake of writing books. I've never, ever wanted to do that. As I said to you, I don't identify myself as a writer necessarily. So, if it took me the rest of my life to write this book, that would be okay.'

Finally, I agreed.

ACKNOWLEDGEMENTS

Without Robyn Davidson's generosity and kindness – occasionally under trying circumstances – this book would not have been possible. Grace is one of her defining qualities, and it was maintained whenever my questions trod onto sensitive territory.

Esther Nunn, James Young and Michelle Arrow threw light onto areas that were occluded to me. I'd also like to thank my wife, Loulou; my editor, Julia Carlomagno; my publisher, Chris Feik; and my agent, Alexandra Christie, who, along with Nicholas Shakespeare, provided invaluable advice at an impasse.

My predecessors in the Writers on Writers

series have my gratitude as well. They surveyed terrain through which I could set my own path, and it is an honour to travel in their company.

WORKS BY ROBYN DAVIDSON

NON-FICTION

Tracks (1980)

Australia: Beyond the Dreamtime (with Thomas
Keneally and Patsy Adam-Smith, 1987)

Travelling Light (1993)

Desert Places (1996)

*No Fixed Address: Nomads and the Fate
of the Planet* (2006)

*Self-Portrait with Imaginary Mother:
A Reluctant Memoir* (forthcoming)

FICTION

Ancestors (1989)